Speed Reading

Dale Owen

CONTENTS

INTRODUCTION

Congratulations on downloading *Speed Reading,* and thank you for doing so.

The following chapters will discuss everything that you may need to know to get started with speed reading. Speed reading is one of the best life skills that you can learn. It will help you to take in more information quickly, allowing you a chance to communicate better with others, and also improve the time in which you can work.

You will also find with speed reading, that reading will actually become a much more enjoyable experience rather than an arduous task.

This guidebook is going to spend some time talking about speed reading and how it can benefit you in your daily life. We will take a look at what speed reading is all about, how you can benefit from speed reading, some of the different techniques that come with speed reading, common mistakes, and even how to increase your comprehension during your speed reading sessions. That is one of the neat things about speed reading. It isn't just about seeing how fast you can get through a page. When you work on it slowly and try to improve your reading speed at a gradual pace that works for you, your comprehension levels of the material will actually also improve aswell.

We will also spend some time talking about subvocalization and how it can be the number one reason that you can't increase your reading speed and see results. Then this guidebook will end with some information on how to improve your reading speeds and some case studies to show you just how effective speed reading can be for your needs.

There are so many great benefits to speed reading. It can enhance your personal and your professional life and is one of the best skills that you can work on for yourself.

There are plenty of different books on this subject available on the market, so thanks again for choosing this one! Every effort was made when making this book to ensure it is full of as much useful information as possible. Please enjoy!

Chapter 1

WHAT IS SPEED READING?

Reading is an activity that can engage a lot of different parts of the body including the brain, mouth, ears, and eyes. When we talk about speed reading, we are looking at a process that is able to engage these senses even more than normal. You will learn how to use the senses, as well as your brain, more efficiently and powerfully than ever before. Speed reading has many different factors to consider when implementing, and getting the most out of your reading times, can make a big difference in the experience you have. Let's take a look at what speed reading is all about!

The Basics of Speed Reading

The first step that you will take when you are ready to read anything is to take a look at the words. But how do you see the words that are on the page when you are reading? Before the 1920s, it was believed that individuals would just go through and read out one word at a time. They thought that to read, you had to move your eyes from left and then over to the right, going across the page. This required you to take in one word after another. With this theory, individuals who were faster readers were simply those who could see and recognize words faster than others.

However, even as a beginner in reading, you can see and then read more than one word at a time. Reading isn't just a smooth transition or flow. You will move the eyes across the page, but it is common to see a lot of jumping ahead in more of fits and starts, taking in between one to five words at a time with just a quick glance. This is normal reading behavior, even though we may not even realize that we are doing it.

The neat thing about speed reading is that it is able to take these natural stops and goes, and clustering of words, and turns it into a method to help you read faster. You already read several words just with one glance. This is true even in regular reading. You may only stop if you come across a word that you don't know as you try to figure that one out.

Speed reading will also help you to expand your vision. Most people who don't use speed reading can take in between one to five words. A speed reader could take in twenty words or more with a single glance, which is why they are able to get through something so much faster.

The expanding of the vision isn't just vertically though. You will find that with speed reading, you are able to expand out your vision to read horizontally as well. In addition to being able to take in more than one word when you read some text, a speed reader has worked on the ability to read and understand the words on different lines, all in the same glance. Isn't it amazing what our minds can do with a little bit of time and practice!

When you read, you may find that you speak the words to yourself. This can be done out loud or in your head. This is the way that we are used to reading things because we were taught the sound it out a method of reading in school. We were taught how to sound out letters and do combinations to read out any word we saw. When we are able to sound out these words, we can learn how to read better.

The problem with this approach is that it is going to slow you down when it comes to reading. You are going to read more at the speed that you talk, rather than at any other speed. Sounding it out with words is fine for those just learning how to read, but it is important to learn when to get rid of this so that you can eventually read faster. People usually don't speak very fast, so using this as your limit to speed reading means you will be done without improving anything.

When you say and hear the words that you are reading, this is going to be known as vocalizing. Vocalizing is something that you will have learned way back when you first got started with reading, which may have helped you in getting started. But it is time to abandon that when you are ready to be a speed reader. One of the things that you will need to work on when learning how to speed read is to shut off that internal vocalization, so it doesn't slow you down.

Another thing to consider is that speed reading is all about comprehending what you read. How well you are able to comprehend what is going on in the document is going to be determined through a variety of factors including how familiar you are with the subject matter, how big your vocabulary is, and your reading speed.

You may be surprised to learn that speed reading is actually a method you can use that will increase reading comprehension. Because you will learn how to read a few words at a time with this method, you will have better luck with learning the meaning of words based on their context. Speed reading, due to this fact, can have a big effect on the size of your vocabulary and your general knowledge, which then turns around and increases your reading speed.

All forms of reading are going to require you to concentrate. Some will require it for longer than others, but to get the message out of the writing, then you need to be able to concentrate. You will find that with speed reading, it is required that you have a sustained, forceful concentration on the material. This is because you are doing a ton of things at the same time, and by doing this effectively, you need to have a good amount of concentration.

To speed read well, you need to see and read the words that are in front of you. Remain alert to the main ideas that the author is trying to send out to you. Learn how to think in the same manner as the author, and detect the method she uses to present the material. That way, it is easier to find out where they put the main ideas. You also need to be able to read with a type of perspective to separate out the details from some of the heavier and more important things. You also need to be able to tell when you can skim, when you should read fast, and even when you need to slow down so you can catch more if you get confused.

Speed reading is one of the best ways to increase your productivity, ensure that you have something to talk about with others, help you to stay on top of changing industry standards, and so much more. It may take some time to learn more about how to use it, but it can definitely be an asset to learn the skills that go with it.

The Benefits of Speed Reading

Speed reading can actually be very beneficial to you. It isn't just about showing off to others that you can read through the newspaper or a document or a book in no time at all. It is also a way to help you comprehend what you are reading and helping you retain the information more effectively.

There are many ways that speed reading can help to improve your life. To start with, many people who properly use speed reading find that it can do wonders for improving the memory. The brain is just like any of the other muscles in the body. If you spend time training the brain, it is going to get stronger and will be able to perform better. One of the neat things about speed reading is that it is going to give our brains a challenge, forcing it to perform at a higher level than usual.

When you use speed reading as a tool to train the brain to take on information faster than before, you will find that all areas of the brain are able to improve, including the memory. When you use the memory in reading it can act like a stabilized muscle. When you speed read, it is going to get in a good workout as you move along, helping you to improve the memory all in one.

Another benefit that you may be able to enjoy when it comes to speed reading is better focus. Reading speed is calculated by words per minute (also known as wpm) The average reading speed for most people is about 200-300 wpm, but in some cases people that speed read can hit a staggering 1200 words per minute. But why is there such a big gap between these groups?

There are two main reasons why we find this kind of gap. The first one is that the reading styles that we are taught when we were younger are not the most efficient. The second is because we lack focus. While we can't do much about the way we were taught to read, we can try to override them with some of the techniques that we will discuss later on. But if we can't focus on what we are reading in front of us, our minds will start to wonder, and we will easily think about other things rather than the content. Speed reading can help build up the focus instead.

Some people often find that when they become an experienced speed reader, they are able to increase their levels of self-confidence. This may be because you can learn anything that you want in a short amount of time with a good level of speed reading skill. Sure, it won't be an absolute amount of learning, but it could be enough to help you prepare when you need to talk with or meet with someone new. This can keep you from stumbling along for topic ideas, and also make interactions with others much easier.

When you take the time to improve your ability to read, and therefore learn, faster, you will find that a lot more doors are going to start opening up for you because there are more options in your life. This is since every book or articles, regardless of whether they are nonfiction or fiction, can help us shift our awareness and we may be able to see more in depth about our lives. This is going to help us see a boost in our own self-confidence.

Reading is a very good exercise that you can do for the brain. When you train the brain not just to read the words, but also read them faster, something amazing can happen. The brain will become more efficient when it is time to sort through information and find correlations to other information bits that you stored in the past.

The more that you are able to improve the reading speed, the faster this process is able to happen. As a side effect of this, you will start to notice some big improvements with logic because you get used to responding quickly to what before would have taken a lot longer to process.

And finally, reading can help improve your personal and emotional wellbeing. Reading is relaxing for most people in general. It can help to reduce the amount of stress that you have because it ensures that you are able to get your mind off your worries, and of the other thoughts you have that may not be beneficial or healthy.

When you can reduce the stress and hide the negative thoughts, this will help you to focus mostly on the information that you take in through reading. This can be a form of meditation that is known as an active meditation. With this type of meditation, you get the same benefits of normal meditation and get into the same kind of state, but whilst doing an activity. It also provides you with an increase in emotional wellbeing and a release of tension.

Speed reading isn't just going to be about learning how to read faster. Think of it more like an exercise. When you exercise the brain, just like you do with your muscles, it is going to start getting significantly stronger over time. This can provide you with all of the benefits that we have stated previously.

Do Speed Reading Programs Really Work?

Speed reading is something that interests many people. They often want to increase their speed but at the same time avoid wasting time trying to get through all the content they are trying to read. When they first start looking through some of their options for speed reading, they encounter tons of different options online that promise to make them fast at reading in just a few weeks, or even less. These types of promises sound attractive to people and usually tempt people into trying them.

However, there can be some problems that come with this. First, many of these programs cost a lot of money. They make big promises that they will be able to help you read in no time, but often these promises do come with really big price tags, sometimes in the thousands of dollars. But is it really worth this much to increase the speed at which you are able to read?

Many times, these courses are going to fail. They won't be able to teach you anything. Sure, you may feel like you are making some progress, but you do all of the work on the computer screen with words flashing at you and praising you for not actually doing that much. Then, when you go back to trying to read a regular document, your comprehension and your reading speed start to go down again.

Even with the programs that are successful at helping you to increase your reading speed, you will find that all the techniques that they teach you are the same ones that we teach inside this guidebook. While these techniques are really great and can increase your speed, the programs that cost hundreds or even thousands of dollars aren't much more impressive overall, and just cause you to throw lots of money away.

Speed reading may be a skill, but that doesn't mean you have to pay a premium to get the benefits out of using it. You can utilize your finger or a pen and a variety of reading materials and do well. Add in some methods that help you count how quickly you are able to read through, so you can test yourself on occasion, and you are set to go.

Does it Take A Long Time to Do Well with Speed Reaching?

When you first get started with speed reading, you are probably really excited to see your reading speed increase and go to new heights. You are excited to see some of the benefits that come with speed reading and how it can benefit your life. But one question that you may still have is how speed reading actually is going to work and how long it takes to see improvements.

There are some factors to consider when it comes to speed reading. Everyone is going to progress at a different rate. Some people may have more time to devote to their practice, and others may find it hard to sit down and practice at all. Some people may have a pretty fast reading level to start with, while others may start out at a slower pace. Understanding what goes into speed reading and why it may take you a bit longer to reach your success, or your goal, compared to others, can help you to make the best use of your time and can give you a good idea of how long it will take to see the results.

The first thing to consider is your current reading speed. If you are already considered a fast reader now, then you will progress through the speed reading techniques faster than others. You may already know some of the methods and are using them in your own reading already, but now you just need to improve upon it a little bit more to get better results and to become even faster.

But then there are those who are slower readers. It takes them a long time to get through any type of reading assignment and maybe they even feel miserable when they have a large book or document to read through. These individuals will have to practice more, and it may take longer for them to get the results they want with speed reading.

And of course, some people fall everywhere between these two levels. Your reading level when you start can have a significant influence on how successful you will be with speed reading and how long it will take you.

Don't compare yourself to others here because you never know where they started out. You may be behind a few people, but you are so much further ahead of others as well.

Another significant determinant of how long it takes to do well with speed reading is how much time you dedicate to practicing, and how consistent you stay with it. If you sit down and spend half an hour each day on some of the techniques that we discuss in this guidebook, and you work hard on your speed reading, you will find that you improve very quickly. But if you only devote a few minutes here and there or you only practice once every few weeks, you are not giving yourself the practice that you need to do well.

If you want to see some great results with speed reading, you must make sure that you give it the time, attention, and practice that it needs. This ensures that you are going actually to get enough practice so that you can get better. The speed reading progress isn't going to happen just because you want it to. It will happen because you dedicate yourself, and remain consistent, with the work that needs to be done.

Speed reading can benefit you in so many ways. It can help you to communicate with people more intelligently. It can help you to be more educated and informed about the information that is the most important to you. Learning some of the best techniques to speed up your reading and to help you take in more information can be one of the best life skills that you learn.

Chapter 2

THE SPEED READING SHORTCUT – STEPS TO MAKE SPEED READING EASIER

Speed reading doesn't have to be a process that is hard and complicated to work on. In fact, you may find that it is a straightforward process if you take a moment to learn about it. Many people may feel that they will never catch on to the secrets that come with speed reading, and that they should just give up now before they end up making themselves tired and frustrated. But in reality, a few minutes a day, along with some of the techniques that we will talk about in a bit, can be enough to ensure that you will see some results with how quickly you can read through various materials. This chapter is going to provide you with some shortcuts you can take, as well as the best steps, to make your speed reading a reality.

Stop the Subvocalization

This is the hardest thing that you are going to work on when you get started with speed reading. Because of the way that we are taught how to read, we often limit ourselves because we think out the words that we are reading, rather than just reading through them and comprehending them. What this does is slows us down to only being able to read as fast as we can talk. This keeps us around 250 words per minute and no more, which is definitely not speed reading.

How can you do this? A good trick to work on is to pick out any word in any text that you want, and then look at it for a moment, staying silent. There may be a bit of subvocalization that comes with it because that is what we are used to, but by merely taking in words without the desire to pronounce them, we are practicing the skills that we need to help out with this problem.

After being able to do this with individual words, just taking them in without the need to pronounce them or sound them out in our heads, you will start to form a new habit of taking in the word and understanding it,

even if you are moving faster. It may take a lot of practice, but over time, you will be able to limit the amount of subvocalization that occurs when you read.

Figuring Out your Current Starting Point

Another element that you need to consider when it comes to working with speed reading is the ability to recognize when you have grown and are doing better than before. Before you are able to figure out this growth though, you need to be able to measure your reading against a baseline. This means that you need to test your reading speed before you even begin, and then test it again at consistent intervals during the training to see how you are doing.

There are a lot of great resources online that you can use that will help you track these results. For example, ReadingSoft.com works well because it will provide you with a quick and consistent measurement of how fast you are reading through some material. When you regularly take reading tests, whether it is through that site or another one, you will be able to see when you are improving your skill, and this is often the motivation that you need to keep things going.

The problem that comes with understanding your own baseline is that it becomes hard for you to translate it into practical terms when you see how many words per minute you are able to read. It is a great place for you to start, but from a practical view, it is important to know the number of minutes it can take to read through a page.

For most people, it can take about 5 to 10 minutes to get through a single page. But for a speed reader, two or three minutes can be enough. This means that for a speed reader, a book that is 200 pages long should take them about 400 minutes to read. But for the average reader, this same book could take between 1000 and 2000 minutes to read. The average reader will spend an extra 13 hours reading a book than a speed reader would, which adds up to a tremendous amount of time which ideally could be reduced.

Using Indicators

We are going to talk about this one in a bit more detail later on, but it is one of the best techniques to use when you are practicing your speed reading. Using a finger to make sure that you are guiding yourself is something that we see a lot of children do as they learn how to read, but since you are learning a new skill as well, it is definitely something that you can utilize too.

The pointer is useful for pushing you along more than helping you keep your place. It is easy to become fixated on a word or phrase when we are reading, and then this slows down our time. When we set a pace with our finger, we force ourselves to move along, without looking back at all, so we can keep up and increase our speed.

The guide needs to be moved at a pace that is very consistent. You never want to go through and stop the finger or try to slow it down. It simply needs to slide from one side of the text over to another at a uniform speed. When you practice using your pointer finger in this manner, you will notice that any time you get stuck or lose momentum much easier than if you simply tried to follow along and move as quickly as possible.

When you just try to go through things and move as quickly as you can, the fluid motion that you need to attain while speed reading isn't possible. You are eventually going to hit a limit, and you will end up skipping words. This causes backtracking, and that results in a lot of confusion. If you do this just two times on each page, it could add in 30 seconds or more per page, or an additional 100 minutes for a book that is 200 pages. That is an extra 90 minutes to finish a book. Just by learning how to reduce how many times this happens, you can increase the speed at which you read by.

Focus on Control

When you are moving through your text, you may find that there are certain parts of the book that are easy for you just to breeze through, but then there are some that are much too full of information that you will need to learn, causing you to slow down and take it all onboard. This is a pretty natural part of reading, and being able to transition smoothly from the easy to read material to the thick material is something that you need to learn how to control. Always remember that speed isn't the only important part of speed reading. You must also take the time to do the actual reading as well.

Let's take a look at two different books to help you see how this works. The first book that we will look through is a thick and boring textbook about history. If we wanted to be able to find specific dates and names inside of this book, it would be pretty easy just to speed read through all of the pages and then scan for the information that we need. If we wanted to find out the significance of the dates and the people, we would skim until we found the information we need, and then slow down to learn about those people and dates. This is a measure of control that we need to work on.

With the second example, the book is going to be one of fiction. This is more about a whimsical story where a family has become trapped on a mountain, and the story follows all the adventures that they have whilst they try to stay clear of danger. Because the brain enjoys this fictional piece, there is no real reason to have much control over this process of reading, unless we find that we don't understand some part of the story. We can go through the text pretty quickly and let the story fill up our mind. If we feel there is something significant or something we missed out on, then we can choose to slow down if we think it's needed. Otherwise, we can just keep reading through the material at any speed that we want.

Doing Exercises to Minimize Eye Movement

One of the biggest things that you can do when you work to speed read is to learn how to minimize the number of movements your eyes make when you are reading. If you are able to start paying attention to how often the eyes are moving when you read, then you will be able to help limit it a bit. This can add hours back to the reading experience and can make the reading time easier to handle.

There are a lot of different exercises that you can work with when it comes to helping your eyes to get stronger and to work on how many movements the eyes need to do. When you do these exercises, you are able to isolate the core components of using your eyes to speed read. You can get more words into each glance, and can also prevent backtracking overall so you can make your reading speeds faster.

Skipping Small and Unimportant Words

To help you figure out the best way to become a speed reader and how they are able to get through pages so quickly while the rest of us struggle, it is important to realize that not every word on the page is equal to each other. There are a lot of smaller words on the page that help with grammar and are important to make sure the sentence flows, but they don't really add much to the sentence at all. For example, take a look at any sentence and remove the words "The, An, A, And." You can still read through that sentence and get the understanding of what is inside it.

If you are able to learn how to eliminate all of these small and irrelevant words, you will find that you are more effective at getting more out of the page and fully understanding what is going on with that page. When you skip these small words, they are not translating to anything that is useful. This allows you to spend more time looking at the information that you need, rather than wasting it on all those small words. And since many times, those small words take up half or more of the words on the page. When you are able to eliminate them, imagine how much more you are able to get done in a shorter amount of time.

The process of training yourself to skip these small words is as simple as recognizing that you don't really need to pay all that much attention to them. Simply allow the eyes to move across and not focus on those unnecessary words. This can take some time, to do. You have to train your eyes to skip over these words, which isn't as easy as it sounds as we are used to seeing them and reading each of them. Over time though, with some practice, your brain is going to learn how to skip over these words for you naturally. This allows you to just read the most important words on the page causing you to read that slight bit faster then usual.

Using some Programs for Help

While you shouldn't spend a lot of money on these apps and programs because you can do a lot of the work on your own, you may find that using a few speed reading apps and programs can help you out. The best tools that you use for speed reading are simple, common apps that are going to help you streamline the process of learning the skill.

There are a few options that you get to choose from. And most of them are going to provide excellent features that make using them both an exercise in speed reading, and a way to save time. One option that you may like if you use IOS 8 is the Accelerator. This one is able to import documents, articles, and any other texts and links that you need into the speed reading practice app. This helps you practice and learn because you are adding in articles that you already are looking at reading, which can make the practice much more engaging and entertaining.

Another option is to work with Spreeder. This is a tool that will help you to copy and paste any kind of text that you want into its small word processor. The app will then take whatever has been pasted and turn it into an exercise so that you can pick and choose what you would like to read and practice all on one app. Spritz App can be a good one as well because it doesn't work the same with teaching you how to read faster. It works to use the software to reconfigure the things that you want to read in a new way. This one is more about not moving the eyes. It is going to flash the words in front of the eye, highlighting one letter to center the word to keep the eyes tracking as they flash by fast.

These are just a few of the options that you can choose. But look around and find one that is free or very inexpensive. These are just supposed to be tools in helping you out. The options that promise to be full courses are often not effective and can cause issues with spending too much and not seeing the improvements as you would like with your reading skills.

Skimming and Scanning

Two main methods are used when it comes to speed reading. The first one is to use your pointer finger or another tool to help move you along and avoid issues with fixation. The second one is skimming and scanning. We will take some more time to look over this as we progress through this guide. But basically, you will use some different techniques to help you get through the text faster, stop reading each and every word, and still get the meaning that you need from the text.

Skimming will allow you to search for some of the main keywords that you need to get through the text faster. If it is a topic that you already know a lot about, then you can simply look for the main topics and keywords that are needed to understand the material. You can then glance through the material and find these important parts and see if there is any new information or something that you may need to focus more of your attention on, rather than having to read through the whole thing.

There are a lot of different things that you can do when it comes to skimming and scanning to get the most out of work. You can take some time to preview the material, such as looking at any summaries or taking a look at the front or the back cover of the document, such as if its a book. You can choose to look at the chapter headings and the subheadings along the book to see what topics will be discussed. Some people even find that reading the first few paragraphs and then just the first lines of each paragraph can help them to get enough information without needing to read each word.

Consistent Practicing Schedule

If you have come this far in the speed reading process, well done. You already have all the tools and the information needed to get a handle on the process and work on developing your skill. It may seem in the beginning that speed reading is a really difficult skill to master, but it isn't as hard as you may think. With just a few key parts being understood and a lot of practice, you are sure to get this all mastered in no time at all.

From this stage, your biggest goal is going to be to find regular and consistent times to continue practicing the techniques that we talked about above, and that we are going to talk about in the rest of this guide. You don't have to give yourself a ton of time to master these skills. But if you never practice at all, or just practice a bit here and there and never on a consistent basis, you will struggle to improve this skill at all. Even fifteen minutes a day can be enough to enhance your reading speed and can make this a skill that is easy to utilize.

Chapter 3

CALCULATING YOUR READING SPEED

Before we get into some of the techniques that you can use to increase your speed, it is important to have a basic idea of how fast your reading speed is in the beginning. How are you supposed to know how far you have come in all of this if you don't know where you began? This chapter is going to take some time to look at how you can calculate your own reading speed. There are also a few different options you can find online that can help you do this automatically.

Once you do the reading test, make sure that you keep the number somewhere safe that you can find later. At regular intervals, whether it's every week or each month which ever works best for you, take another speed test. You can then compare the two numbers and see how far you have come. This is a great way to keep you on task with your speed reading goals, and when you get stuck or feel like you aren't progressing, you can compare these numbers and see how far you have really come.

Calculating your Reading Speed

Here we are going to give you a simple formula that is easy to work through to figure out your reading speed. You also have a choice to use some of the tests online to figure out your reading speed if you so choose. The steps that you can use to figure out your own reading speed, and to see where you are starting this journey include:

> ➢ Take out a document or a book or something else to read. Turn on a timer for five minutes and just read at your normal pace.
> ➢ When the time is up, mark the spot where you stopped.
> ➢ Count the number of words that are found in the first five lines that you read. Divide this number by five, so you get the average words per line.
> ➢ Then Count the number of lines that you read.

➤ Then Multiply this by the number of lines that you read by average on each line. This is a rough estimate of how many words you have ended up reading during that five minutes.

➤ Now Divide it by five, so you know how many words per minute you were able to do.

Since this one doesn't have a set number of words for you to read through, it may be a little bit off. But it is a good method to go with to teach you how these words per minute are calculated. You can also choose to pick out a document with a known number of words and then time how long it takes to read that normally. Divide the total number of words by how much time it took to get your words per minute.

The goal is to see if you can get faster than this first time. Write that number down someplace safe, and then, when you have had some time to practice and get better at speed reading, you can go through the above test again and see if you have gotten faster. You may be surprised by how much you improve each time that you do the test. Keep records so you can always look back and see how far you have come.

Average Reading Speed

For most people, the average reading speed is going to be about 200 words per minute, or slightly higher. This allows them to comprehend what they are reading, but it also shows that quite a bit of subvocalization is going on as well. Some readers are able to get around 300 words per minute, but this number is pretty low.

The goal is to get yourself to 1000 words per minute or more. If you are done at 200 words per minute right now, this may seem like a crazy goal that you will have trouble meeting. But even those who read at a slower speed can use speed reading to improve their skills. You can start out at any level, and using some of the techniques that we will talk about later will help improve your speed. Even if you just can't manage to get to 1000 words per minute, improving your reading speed by even a couple hundred words per minute can make a big difference.

Word-per-Minute

There are a lot of different reading speeds to watch out for. Sometimes it depends on what level of reading you are at (beginners are going to be slower at reading compared to older adults), and other factors. Below is a good idea of what a word per minute can mean depending on the level you are at:

➢ 1 to 100 words per minute: This is the speed that we often see beginners and children reading out. This is considered the borderline of literacy. There is little recollection or even understanding of the material that is read. But the person is beginning to read, so it usually gets better.

➢ 100 to 200 words per minute: This one is going to still fall below average, and many people who fall in this range find that they don't enjoy the reading at all. It is difficult for them to read to learn and stay up to date on any changes occurring around them. Many times, their comprehension of the material will still be under 50 percent, even if they are older.

➢ 200 to 250 words per minute: Many people are going to fall somewhere between this range. This is the average speed for reading. But if you are re-reading the words and trying to subvocalize them, then your reading comprehension can still be down at fifty percent.

➢ 250 to 300 words per minute: This number of words per minute is going to be just a bit above range, and there are a lot of post-high school graduates that will use this kind of speed. But you will find that the comprehension will still stay around fifty percent.

➢ 350 to 500 words per minute: This is the range that is above average by quite a bit, and the ones who fit into this category of speed are the ones who typically enjoy spending their time reading. The retention of these individuals can be good, and it falls somewhere between 50 to 75 percent. This is good reading speed, but you will find as we go through this book, you can do much better.

➢ 500 to 800 words per minute: This is fast reading speed. These individuals enjoy reading quite a bit and are starting to fall into the speed reading category. These people are often the ones who will spend their free time curled up with a book rather than watching a movie.

➢ 800 to 1000 words per minute: This is efficient reading speed. You should be able to use this speed and not have to feel pressured or stressed about reading. You will understand lots of words and their meanings well, and you may have even spent some time doing speed reading training along the way. You don't waste your time subvocalizing words or re-reading them.

➢ 1000 words per minute or faster: You have now entered the speed reading area. Being able to read at this speed means that you now have complete control over your reading and you are a master of it. This is considered an elite reading category. Reading is a big part of your life, both for business and for pleasure, so reading at this sort of speed will be highly beneficial to your life in general.

So, the first thing that you need to do here is to take some time to test out your reading speed. You can pick an online test, or you can use the steps that we talked about above. Don't try to speed through the reading or do anything unnatural at this time to try to impress anyone. Doing this is going to mess with your results and makes it hard to see where your baseline truly is. Simply start out by reading at your natural speed and then you can see where your current reading speeds are at.

If you find that your reading speed is a bit lower than you thought, or on the lower end of the spectrum above, don't fret, or be too harsh towards yourself. There is plenty of time to work on your speed reading and to improve it a lot more. You simply are doing these tests to figure out how to speed yourself up; it doesn't really matter how fast or slow the reading is in the beginning. Speed reading can help you to increase your speed, and even if you just increase it by a few hundred words a minute, you will find that your love of reading, and how quickly you can get through things, will increase as well.

Chapter 4

HOW TO READ FASTER

Once you have had some time to look at your reading speed and you know where you want to start, and maybe even have a goal that you would like to reach with this process, it is time to learn some of the techniques that are needed to help you read faster than ever before. Let's take a look at some of the different techniques that you can use to go from your current reading speed to a speed reader in no time.

There are actually quite a few different techniques that you can choose to go with when you want to increase your reading speed. All of them can be effective, but it often depends on who is reading and what works the best for them. Some of the best speed reading techniques that you can try out include:

The Hand Pacing Technique

This is such a simple method to use, and you only need your own hand to get it done. This allows you to read faster while ensuring that you read at a steady pace, so you can get through the document without getting distracted or stopping at different words. Have you ever worked with or heard about someone using the pointer method? Most of us learned how to use this technique when we were in school, but many of us dropped the habit as we got older. But even as of today, it is still an incredibly effective method to use.

Working with hand pacing is pretty easy. You just need your hand, or your finger, and some sort of document to work with. When you are ready and comfortable, you can use these steps to help you get used to speed reading in this way:

- Sit down at a 45-degree angle from the document you are reading. Sit as comfortable as possible, and have your elbow on the table.
- Let one of your hands hold onto the reading material. Then you can use a pointer or the index finger on either hand, whichever is the most comfortable for you.
- Position the pointer under the word that you want to first start with. Start pacing yourself as

you read through the document, moving along the lines and making sure you never fall behind the pointer.

➤ Keep your eyes concentrated on both the pointer and the words that show up in front of you.

➤ The pointer needs to move at a steady pace the whole time that you are reading and doing this exercise. Do not let it slow down and don't let your eyes or the words determine how fast you get to go. The pointer or the finger get to choose the pace.

➤ Try to remember what you can from the document. If you are struggling with comprehension, then you can adjust the speed. But always strive to go faster each time that you practice.

➤ With this method, make sure that you just keep moving. It is fine if you miss a few words here and there. If you are catching most of the document, then this is not going to be an issue. Just keep going, even if you do miss a few words.

When you work on this, your motion should be free-flowing and continuous. If you know the material is going to be more difficult, you can go at a slower pace to help with comprehension. But don't let the pointer slow down just because you feel like it. Coax the brain into going faster and allow it to handle the words and everything else. If you get back into your old habits and notice that you are not self-pacing any longer, just start again!

Scanning and Previewing

Another method that you can go with is the scanning and previewing method. This one will enhance your skills when it comes to capturing the central idea of what you are reading, without wasting time going through all the introductions and all the other stuff that might get in the way. When you use this technique, you may focus your attention on things with lots of information that is condensed so you will learn how to look at subheadings, indexes, graphs, points, and lists to find what you want.

Scanning is a technique that you can use that will trigger and then extract key information and ideas from the document, without having to read the whole thing. You will use scanning simply by moving your eyes quickly down the page, looking for either specific phrases or words to help you get the main idea of that document. You can also use this as a way to figure out whether a source is going to be the one that will answer your questions or not. In many cases, you can use this to get a lot of information out of a document, although not full comprehension, in just a few minutes.

Skimming is a little bit different. This one works well with nonfiction material, and it helps you to focus on the main concept of the document. You will figure out what is the most important parts to the document that you can read. You can choose to stop if you find something that is particularly interesting to you, but the point is to keep on moving and getting through the material.

Previewing key sentences

There are actually a lot of different skimming and scanning strategies that you can use to help increase your reading speed. The first one is going to be previewing key sentences. For this one, you will find the sentences that are at the beginning of a chapter or a paragraph. These are going to give you the basis of what is going to be found in the rest of the writing without having to read through all of it.

Each paragraph is usually going to spend its time on just one idea, though there are sometimes when the paragraphs are going to relate to each other. When you are able to skim and then find out the central idea that is behind each one, you will be able to get the basis or the gist out of it, which aids you in understanding what is in the whole chapter, just by reading a few lines.

You can also go with an approach that is slightly different. You can just look for the information that you need, and then skip the rest. This can help you to read the first and then the last sentence of those longer paragraphs. When you read these two sentences, you learn what the paragraph is about, and how it is summarized. This gives you a ton of information with just a few lines, enabling you to move on to something else quickly.

Scan for any numbers and names

For pretty much every text that you are going to work with, you will find numbers and names inside. These are there to tell you more details about the concepts, places, and people you should pay attention to. There is no order of getting that information in a text during a preview. However, you will find that you can understand some of the main facts of a document, or gain a better understanding of where and when a story takes place or who is involved when you look at numbers.

Scanning for trigger words

The concept with this one is to preview a text, maybe using some of the techniques above. But your goal here is to look for important words that seem to be critical to the document, or ones that seem to keep popping up as you go through the text. Mainly you are going to find compounds or nouns when you are doing this. Some of the trigger words that you may look for will include key sentences, places, names, and numbers.

Reading the title

Always take the time, no matter what method you do, to read through the titles. The title, the content, and the back of the book or text is the most important thing that you can do. This helps prepare you for what will be found in the rest of the document, and may even be able to reveal a few of the trigger words that you need. You can go through and read the titles of the chapters, the headings and subheadings, and any short summaries that show up.

Exercises for skimming and scanning

This is often one of the best techniques that you can use for speed reading when you want to take in a lot of information quickly, without wasting your time and without needing to have a lot of comprehension on the material. Some of the ways that you can practice working on skimming and scanning include:

1) **Key sentence:** For this one, go and grab any book that you like. Take a moment to read through the first sentences or the first few paragraphs that are there. Now try to recall the ideas that your mind grabbed and latched onto when you read through those sentences using the concept that we talked about above. As a beginner, just do this on about four to five sentences. Once you have mastered it on that amount of reading, you can jump ahead and do more.

2) **Names and numbers:** For this one, you can choose any article that you want. Then skim through it and see what numbers or names you are able to find with it. When you find a fact, a number or a name, pause for a few seconds, not very long, and realize it. You can choose to say the word out loud if you would like. Now, start reading through the entirety of the document and see if the facts, those that you paused on, will start to reveal themselves as you go.

3) **Trigger words:** For this one, you can choose a few different books or articles to get started

with. When you have them ready, you can start by reading the titles, the content, the back of the book, and any headlines that you see. From this information, try to write down a few trigger words. When you start speed reading, stop at the words that interest you. Write those words down as well because these are new trigger words to pay attention to. When you are done, see how much information you were able to comprehend from those articles.

Skimming and scanning are great options to go with if you want to be able to read through a lot of information quickly, without having to worry about comprehending everything. This helps you to get the gist out of the information, so you can share the news, or know what is going on, without having to read each individual word.

Reading Groups of Words

Out of all the methods, reading chunks of words is considered the most advanced out of all the techniques. You can also combine it with the others, such as pacing, to move faster. When you use this particular technique, it is going to make it easier for you to process big chunks of words, rather than just going through and reading out the single words that are there. It has been used by many people to fully process the information at hand, rather than having to go through and read slowly through each individual word.

Learning how to read chunks of words is all about training, and it can take some time. You have to learn how to expand out your vision, so you can read a chunk of words at once, and get their meaning, rather than just one. Some of the things that you will need to practice when it comes to reading groups of words include:

- ➢ Extend the vision
- ➢ Combine a few different reading strategies
- ➢ Reduce some of the other bad habits that you have formed when it comes to reading
- ➢ Ignore some of the filler words that are there, but don't really contribute to your comprehension.

- Learn how to focus your attention mainly on verbs and nouns.
- Reduce any stops that are due to eye fixation.

As a beginner, you will want to start out with just chunking together two or three words at a time. While this method can definitely help you become a faster reader, it is sometimes difficult to do. You can go through and just chunk together two or three words in the beginning, and you will instantly see how much faster it is to read. Over time, you may be able to glance down and read a whole paragraph in that single glance, and only take just a few seconds to do so.

The training plan for this one is pretty simple. You can set aside about ten to fifteen minutes a day to help you learn how to recognize many words at the same time while reading. Don't make the training session much longer than this, or implement other methods besides just chunking. This can be a long period, especially for beginners, to spend on just speed reading techniques and can wear you out.

When you start your training, work with just two words chunked together at a time. This is the perfect place to start as a beginner, and it is going to stimulate the brain to process a larger number of words each minute. You don't need to rush or skip up a level until you are able to read the two words at a time smoothly and easily.

You can also add in the pointer method here. Using your index finger to help you go from one group over to another can make it easier to jump around the page without getting fixated on any word. You can also use the pointer to help you go a bit faster to get more stimulation and to ensure that you will be ready to move onto the next level in no time.

We will talk about this in a bit, but you may notice that the issues of subvocalization show up as a beginner to speed reading, which may be the thing that is slowing you down quite a bit. What this means is that while you are doing these exercises, you are trying to pronounce the words in your head, or even by moving your mouth, while you read. This is a bad reading habit that is pretty common, but if you want to progress chunking five words or more, it is one that you need to be aware of, and you need to work on to avoid.

After you master at least four words chunked together in a sentence, you can try to use a hand pacing method that is known as the Zig Zag. With this method, instead of following the lines perfectly, you would go down the page in a zig-zag motion, jumping to different word groups each time. The point of this is to help you skip past all of the words that are just filler, helps you to move faster, and an ensure that you get to the central idea of the document or book much faster than before.

These are some of the main methods that you can use when it comes to increasing your reading speed. As you can see, the ideas are pretty simple, but they will require you to do some work. Even ten to fifteen minutes a day as a beginner can be enough to stimulate the mind and teach it how to read in this manner. Over time and with some persistence and dedication, you will be able to become a speed reader in no time.

Eye Exercises to Improve Reading Speed

In addition to some of the techniques that we discussed above, you should also consider working on your eye movements and eye strength as well. None of the methods that we talk about are going to be that effective if you can't move your eyes fast enough to read through the page and if you aren't able to take in more words at a time with the help of your peripheral vision. Luckily, there are a few different exercises that you can do with your eyes to help you with your speed reading includes:

Thumb-to-thumb glancing

This first method is a good one to use to work the eye muscles and help you to control your peripheral vision. It can also stretch out the muscles of the eyes to make them more flexible and healthier. To work with this kind of exercise, you should glance at your thumbs without moving the head at all. The steps that you can do to work with the thumb to thumb glancing exercise includes:

1) Sit or stand, whichever is the best for you, and look straight ahead without turning your head at all. Then stretch the arms out to your sides, letting the thumbs stick out.

2) Without letting the head turn at all, glance back and forth between the left and the right thumbs, doing this ten times.

3) Repeat these steps a few times to work on the peripheral vision and to make your eyes stronger.

This is an exercise that you can add in at the beginning of each of your practices to ensure that you are able to see your eyes get a bit stronger. It only takes a few minutes at most, and you will start to notice a lot of improvements to your reading speed in no time.

Eye writing

The second exercise that you can work with is known as eye writing. With this exercise, you are going to move your eyes in ways that it may not be used to working with. The eye gets used to seeing things in a certain way. These muscles are well trained, but you may want to strengthen them a bit with the help of moving your eyes differently than they are used to. This gives them a workout, and may make the muscles a little bit sore in the beginning, but can be really worth it for improving your reading speed.

The eye writing exercises that we are going to talk about will work on the extra-ocular muscles that are in the eye socket, and it is perfect for helping increase the amount of flexibility in the eye as well as its range of motion. It is a simple process though, you just need to use the steps below to help you get started:

1) Find a blank wall that you are able to do this with. Try to sit across the room from it, or as far away as you can from that wall.
2) When you are ready, stare at the wall and imagine that you are writing your name on that wall. You will move the eyes around as you would with a paintbrush like you were writing the name that way.
3) You can try writing out your name in a few different manners. You can do it in block letters, uppercase and then lowercase, and even in cursive.

You can do this with any kind of word that you want. Only do it a few times the first few exercises that you do it to help you get the basics, but your eyes will get tired in the beginning. Over time, you will see improvement, and you will find yourself being able to do more complex words, and for a longer period of time. This is another one that you can bring into the beginning of your speed reading practice to ensure that you stretch the eyes out a bit and can help you read a bit faster.

Hooded eyes

Now we are onto the third exercise that you can work on. This exercise is going just to take a few seconds, and works the best when you have been speed reading for a bit, and you need to give the eyes a little break from work. Sometimes we get into some of our speed reading a little too much, but then our eyes get tired and worn out in the process. Hooded eyes are a great way to relax your eyes a bit so that they don't strain too much, and you can use it in the middle of the practice to help you keep going for longer, or at the end of the session as well. To work with the hooded eyes, you can use the following steps:

59

1) Close your eyes, just halfway. You should concentrate on trying to keep the eyelids from trembling in the process. While you spend this time concentrating on the eyelids, you are really working on relaxing the eyes a little bit, which can be super relaxing and helps with the strain that you may be feeling after speed reading for a bit.

2) Once you have gotten the eyelids to quit trembling, you can keep the eyes half closed, and gaze at some faraway object. You will notice that as you do this, your eyes are going to stop trembling a little bit.

Eye squeezes

And the final exercise that we are going to take a look at to help improve the strength of our eyes is known as eye squeezes. This is another exercise that you can work with that are going to relax the muscles of the eyes, while also helping you to make these muscles more flexible, and can increase the amount of oxygen and blood that is able to flow to the eyes and the face. Not only does this help you improve your eye strength for easier speed reading, but it can also keep wrinkles away and make you look younger!

This exercise may take a little longer than what you will find with the other types of exercise, but it is still a good one to try out every once in a while, to ensure that you are working on your eyes and keeping them healthy and strong at the same time. Some of the things that you can do to help you get started on the eye squeeze exercise include:

1) As you inhale, going deep and slow, open your eyes and mouth as wide as you can. Work on stretching out each and every muscle in your face.

2) As you exhale, close and squeeze the eyes as tightly as you can. At the same time, you want to make sure that you are also squeezing in all of the muscles of the head, neck, and face. You should also clench the jaws a bit.

3) Hold the breath out for 30 seconds, making sure that you squeeze everything for that whole time. This may be hard in the beginning, but

with some practice, you will be able to do it and really work on those muscles well.

4) Repeat the steps above another four times. If you need to, take a short break in between them. If you are able to do so, take another break and then do another set of five to really work on the muscles. If you can't do more, at least get through that original set of five to work on the muscles, and then work up from there.

Since this exercise usually takes a bit longer to work on and complete than some of the others, it doesn't need to be done each time, unless you are setting aside half an hour or more for your practice. But it is still a good one to work on, or implement, into your practice at least once a week. It provides so many benefits to your whole face and all of the muscles that you use while reading, especially when it comes to speed reading.

All of these great eye exercises are going to enhance what you are able to do with some of the other techniques that we discussed in this chapter. You should consider doing at least one or two at the beginning or the end of each speed reading session.

This will ensure that you are able to get the best results out of the process and when your eyes get stronger, you will be able to skim and use the other techniques to their full potential.

When you are practicing your speed reading, you will need to do a bit of experimenting to find out which technique is going to work the best for you. Each person is going to work in a slightly different manner than others, so you will need to try out a few different kinds to ensure that you are able to get the one that works the best for you. And once you find the technique that clicks for you, your reading speed will increase in no time.

Chapter 5

WHERE PEOPLE GO WRONG WITH SPEED READING

Speed reading can be a very easy way for you to make sure that you can get through a lot of information in a short amount of time. There are a lot of great techniques that you are able to work with to help you increase your speed, and these will help you to get through a lot of material in a short amount of time, while also increasing your comprehension at the same time.

However, some mistakes can be made when it comes to working on speed reading. Learning how to avoid these mistakes can make a big difference in how successful you are with speed reading. Let's take a look at some of the ways that people may go wrong when they first get started with their own speed reading journey.

Common Mistakes with Speed Reading

Learning to do speed reading can be a huge time saver, and it can even help you to benefit your academic or professional career tremendously. However, if you are going through speed reading and you fall prey to some of the common reading mistakes, then you are going to miss out on some of the great benefits that come with it. Some of the most common mistakes that you can see when it comes to speed reading includes:

Reading through everything at the same speed

When you are first learning how to speed read, you may assume that you must read each and everything that you see at the same speed. This mistake can be hard to avoid because many readers are going to use their finger or hand to help guide their eyes. Because they do this, they will end up going line by line, staying at the same speed. This can sometimes seem like they fall into a rhythm, regardless of what they are reading.

Working this way doesn't make a lot of sense. Not everything that you read about is going to be equally important. You will quickly find that you can go through a document and find some sentences, and some paragraphs, that are going to be more important than the others. You can speed through some of the simple stuff and then slow down when it comes to some of the more important things.

There are a few ways that you can make sure that you are able to adjust your reading speed. This makes your reading more efficient to ensure that you are reading to get the most comprehension possible. Some of the things that you can do to adjust your speed include:

> **Adjusting the speed to fit the type of material you are reading:** You should speed up on any of the material that is easier to get through, such as magazines, and then slow down the speaking a bit on material that may be a bit more technical, such as what is found in textbooks. This ensures that you can keep up with the material and understand what is going on no matter the situation. Besides, if you are already pretty familiar with the material and

what is inside, you can push yourself to get through it faster.

> **Adjust the speed to fit your purpose:** If the purpose of doing the reading is just to get to know the basics of content or material, then you don't need to slow down. Try to fly through that material as fast as possible. But if you need to go through and get a ton of details, then it wise to take a slower approach to reading.

One of the hardest decisions to make when you are trying to speed through a document is whether you need to speed up or slow down on that particular document. You will learn how to strike this balance a bit better as you get more practice with your speed reading.

Re-reading through unnecessary things

At some point or another, all of us have gone back and re-read some material. But there are many times when this is not necessary because you have gathered all of the information from the start anyway. You should never go back after you just get done with one sentence though. While it is possible that you might not have fully understood that sentence, it is also possible that the following one will clear things up. You may even need to finish out the paragraph to fully understand what is being said.

You don't want to waste your time going through and re-reading the whole paragraph or sentence each time. As you skim through and do the other reading techniques, you will quickly find that you are able to catch the majority of what is being said as long as you just keep going.

If you are prone to re-reading the things that are in your documents, then this is one of the first things that you need to work on fixing to see some results. To help with this, start out with a smaller document. Speed read through it with some of the techniques that we have talked about, and force yourself to read through the whole thing, without going back and trying to re-read it. You may find that just pushing yourself forward and not letting yourself look backward, perhaps with a piece of paper over the things you already read, and see just how much you are still able to comprehend at the end.

Poor concentration

When trying to increase your reading speed, you must have a lot of good focus. Poor concentration can destroy the comprehension that you have, regardless of whether you read slowly or fast. The better your concentration, the faster you are able to read. And if you can concentrate well, you may also be able to reach a better comprehension of the material that you are reading. Two simple tips that you can follow to improve your focus includes:

Read with your hand: This is going to help you to focus you by guiding your eyes across the line. If you use a pacer, your hand, or a pen, you will notice that you will keep moving forward, without re-reading the information again. Using your hand to guide is one of the most basic ways to help improve your focus while reading.

Eliminate the distractions: There are some distractions around you that you can actually control.

If you are trying to see if you can focus on the reading better, then it's probably a good idea to make sure that the phone is off. Do you have the urge to check your social media, email, or other texts on your phone when it is time to read? Then turn it all off to help you out. If you can think of any other distractions that can keep you away from your reading, then try to avoid and keep clear when practicing your reading.

Myths with Speed Reading

When you first get started with speed reading, you may have some preconceived notions about what it all entails and what it means. It is common for a lot of people to have these notions as well. But sometimes, these are going to get in the way of you actually seeing success with your own endeavors. Some examples of common speed reading myths include the following:

1) **When you speed read, you don't enjoy reading as much as before.** Many find that when they speed read, they are more efficient as a reader, and then therefore they will get more pleasure and meaning out of the documents

they read. In fact, many get started with speed reading and then develop a love of reading afterward.

2) **You won't do well with comprehending the material.** If you accurately do speed reading, you will find that you are able to comprehend the information just fine. For some people, after practicing speed reading, their level of comprehension usually increases naturally. You will be able to read words in context and then derive more meaning from the words you have read.

3) **You skip words when you do speed reading.**

4) **You have to use a pointer as your pacer to speed read:** This is one of the methods that you can use to speed your reading up a bit. But it isn't always necessary. You can use another tool to help with this or use one of the other methods without relying on your finger or a pointer. That is the beauty of speed reading; you get the freedom with how you choose to do the whole process by picking the method that works the best for you.

5) **Speed reading is hard to do:** Many people assume you need to have special skills to get started with speed reading. They often will think that if they don't have enough reading speed or enough intelligence or something else along the way, that speed reading is something that they are not capable of doing. But anyone is able to work with speed reading. As long as you are ready to put in some work, you are going to see some results with speed reading.

What If I'm Not Improving with Speed Reading?

If you have tried some of the techniques above, and you find that your speed reading just isn't improving as much as you would like, it may be time to change things up. Maybe you are setting your goals too high. It is a great thing to have high goals, ones that are going to challenge you a bit to reach them. But if you want to jump up 300 words a week for the next month, then you are probably putting too much pressure on yourself.

Instead of doing this, set out goals that are realistic and going to work well for you. Maybe try to improve your reading by 100 words a minute for each week for a month. Or find another goal that seems to work the best for you.

You may also find that the technique you are using can cause issues, the place where you are speed reading is too difficult to concentrate in (perhaps because of all the noise), or something else is distracting you and making it difficult to do the reading that you want. Take some time to take a step back and try to see what is causing the trouble or thing that mind be hindering your progress. This is often the best thing to do if your struggling to see any form of progression or improvement.

When and When Not to Use Speed Reading

There are a lot of times when working with speed reading can be a great option to go with. When you want to keep up with the news but don't have a lot of time to read through all the articles and publications, speed reading can be a great option. When you need to find just the information that you need for work or for a report, then speed reading can save you a lot of time because you can skim and see if the article or document is even worth your time. If you just need to glance through a report or another document to make sure that you understand the gist of everything, then speed reading can be helpful.

But there are sometimes when speed reading isn't going to be a good idea. This is mostly when you need to fully understand the document and what is inside, rather than just getting the basics of it. If you have a legal contract, a report from work, or another document that may have a lot of sensitive information in it, and you want to make sure you get all of the information, then you need to actually read through the whole thing rather than chunking or skimming. You still can use speed reading with this type of material, but you don't want to let it become the primary way you read in these situations.

Speed reading is not best used when reading literature either. There is often a lot more plot information, talking and more and speed reading through it can make it more difficult to understand what is going wrong. You can use some of the techniques here, such as reading the chapter headings and the back cover to get some information on what is going to happen next, but for the most part, you will have to read literature at a slower and steadier pace to keep up with everything.

Many great things come with speed reading in your life. But you have to know how to do it the right way. Jumping right in without any preparation or without any idea of how to do the process, or when is the right time to work on the speed reading can just lead you to failure. Avoid some of the common mistakes that are found above, and you will become a speed reading professional in no time.

Chapter 6

COMPREHENSION WHEN SPEED READING

When you get started with speed reading, you may be concerned about whether your comprehension is going to fail. You may have heard stories in the past about others who have tried out speed reading and struggled to make it work. Maybe, they realized that their comprehension got worse, and, that they just couldn't stop subvocalizing.

However, speed reading is not the enemy of comprehension. In fact, if you speed read correctly, you will be able to increase your speed while reading and still understand and comprehend the content being read at the same time. In many cases, your comprehension will get better than it was before. Let's look at some of the particulars of comprehension during speed reading and how you increase your comprehension to get the most out of speed reading.

How Speed Reading Effects Comprehension

Many people think that when your speed reading, your comprehension will go downhill. They think that you will just read too fast to catch what is going on around you and what is in the document. Therefore, there are a lot of people who recommend sticking with regular reading rather than trying speed reading.

If you don't work with speed reading in the right way, and you just try to race through the material without using any of the techniques that we discussed in this guidebook, then you will surely run into issues with comprehension. Too many people like just to pick up a few words to say they got a lot of words done a minute. Doing this cuts down your comprehension because you aren't taking in the important stuff, the stuff that can help them understand what is actually going on in the document.

If you use the right techniques and you focus on speed reading at the right pace based on your skills, then you will actually see that your comprehension will increase with this method. There are several reasons for this.

First, when you have to focus on the words that are in front of you to go quickly, you are less likely to daydream and lose your focus on the material. Since you have laser sharp focus for the material, rather than reading slowly and hoping that your mind doesn't drift off.

Also, speed reading can help you with comprehension because you spend time looking for the material and the information that is actually important. With traditional reading, you will spend your time looking through a lot of information to find what you need. In fact, you may get so caught up in the information that is not needed, that you will often miss out on the important things. This is why, if you do speed reading the right way, you will be able to catch more information and understand more out of each document that you read.

Retaining More Information during Speed Reading

There is no question that learning how to read fast can benefit you in many different ways. Learning to read faster is an important skill, such as learning how to use

78

a computer or different software programs based on your business. This means that you can learn, practice, and improve on your reading speed. But when you are working on your reading speed, it is also important that you learn how to retain more of the information as well. Some tips that you can use to help you to retain the information when speed reading include:

Avoid subvocalization

Subvocalization is a process where you pronounce the words that you read silently in your head as you go. This is something that we do without even realizing it in many cases because this is how we learned how to read. But if you keep going with this process, your reading speed isn't going to get faster. This process is only going to hinder your reading speed and can even distract you from the meaning that is in the text.

Do you know whether you subvocalize or not? The next time that you pick up a document or something to read, take a moment to see if you seem to read the words out loud in your head. The more aware you become with this habit, the easier it can be to break it.

Practice reading faster to make this process a lot harder to do, allowing you to gradually break the habit.

Preview the information you are going to read

It can be harder to comprehend what information is in the text if you have no idea what it is about when you start. Before you go through and read something new, especially if you have no idea what the topic is about and if you find it challenging, then you should review the document first. Take a look at any summaries, who wrote the article, why they wrote it, and what you think the text will have inside.

Track your progress

It is impossible to know if you are even making any progress if you don't know where you got started at. Before you start with any of the techniques that we talk about in this guidebook, make sure that you take a short reading and comprehension test, as we talked about before. This gives you a baseline, to see where your reading level is at the beginning.

From there, you will then get a better idea of the best ways to improve your reading over time. As you work through your own reading and working on improving your speed, you will then be able to compare where you are to where you were, allowing you to see the improvement.

Try not to do these tests too often though. You are working on developing this skill, it isn't something that is going to happen overnight. After about two weeks, then you can go back and use the same test to see if your speed and comprehension are getting better. Try to stick with the same test, so your results are consistent throughout the process.

Learn how to skip the small words

This process isn't quite the same as skimming, but it can be similar, and it really will speed up how quickly you are able to read. Words like "a, the, an, it" and so on don't add a ton to your comprehension and stopping to read them will just slow you down even more.

Don't believe that this works. Go and take out a paragraph and eliminate all of the words that are three letters or less. Then, go through and read through the paragraph. You may notice that it is quite a few of the words in the document. But as you go through and read the words that are left, you will find that you can still get the gist and the basics that come with the document.

Now you can move this over to the other things that you read. Try reading through a whole page, or more, and see if you can skip over some of the smaller words. Even if you haven't perfected the other methods, just skipping over the small words, the ones that don't mean that much, can help you see some results in how fast you can read.

Techniques to Help Comprehend Better through Speed Reading

Being able to speed read is a great skill to have. It can help you to improve and progress your personal and professional life. But being able to read quickly is not the only thing to consider when we work on this skill. You must also comprehend the material that you decide to read. Without this comprehension, you are just wasting your time reading. Some of the tips that you can use when it comes to comprehending the material when you are speed reading includes:

Make sure the distractions are gone

Distractions are going to be your worst enemy when it comes to trying to increase your reading speed. You need to learn what are the biggest distractions for you and how to avoid them to see the best results. For example, most people find that their phones can be a big distraction. If it goes off and makes any noise, such as from a text message, email, or someone calling, their attention will go straight from the task at hand and over to the phone. Turn the phone off and even consider leaving it in another room if you can't keep your focus.

If there is a computer in the room and your planning on practicing, it is time to turn it off and not let it distract you at all. The dings from social media, emails, and other things can easily take your attention away from the reading. Turn the computer off so you can't even see the stuff pop up.

When it is time to practice your speed reading, make sure that you go to a room that is devoid of distractions. Find one that has good lighting, a chair that is comfortable and no distractions. If you can, try to do it at a time when others are not at home to prevent further distractions. You want to be in an environment that allows you to focus just on the speed reading and nothing else.

Slow down just a Little

Yes, we have spent a lot of time in this guidebook talking about speed reading and learning how to increase your words per minute. But if you are reading fast and not comprehending anything that it says, then this speed reading process is not going to be very effective for you. You have to increase your speed realistically, going at a speed that makes the most sense for your skills, not killing yourself to get faster too soon.

You do not want to go from 200 words per minute to 1000 words per minute in a week or so. This may mean that you are taking in more words, but you are definitely not comprehending much, and not taking in what your reading. You have to set goals that are realistic for your needs and your own personal reading level. You will get to 1000 words eventually if you keep working and practicing. But you will not get there in just a few weeks.

If you notice that you are able to increase your words per minute, but you notice that your comprehension goes down or starts getting worse, then you may be jumping ahead too fast. Slow down a little, even just 50 words per minute, and you may find that this is a better level for you to concentrate and comprehend on the information. You can always increase later on with a bit more practice.

Make sure you are well-rested

If you are tired or drowsy, it is much harder for you to concentrate on the material in front of you. You are more likely to fall asleep and read sentences over and over again because you can't even keep your eyes open, much less concentrate on the words that are in front of you on the page.

85

It is best to pick a time of day that you are well rested and can feel renewed, so you can pay more attention. If you feel a bit tired, and like you may get over comfortable in your chair, you may feel yourself glazing over staring at words and not being able to focus. Try taking small breaks when reading, but try not too take too long; fifteen minutes is enough to refresh the body without wasting a lot of time. But if you are really tired it may be a good idea to give it a miss this time round.

Release the stress so you can focus

If you are feeling a lot of stress, then it is going to be hard to focus and concentrate on any document you need to look at, and this makes it even harder to get the comprehension that you need. All of us deal with stress on a daily basis. Our modern world is stressful with thinking about work, school, kids, and everything else that needs to go on and get done. But we are in control over how we manage that stress and we can choose what to do about it.

To release stress, there are many methods that you can choose to help with this. Some people find that going on a regular exercise plan can help them out. Getting in 30 minutes or more of some kind of physical activity, whether it is weight lifting, running, cardio or some form of stretching or yoga, can help you to release a lot of stress, and it is really good for your whole body. Even if you don't have a lot of health goals to reach, exercise can be a great way to help you out, as it can also help to clear the mind enabling your reading to improve.

Others may find that journaling is a better option for them to go with. They can spend even ten minutes at the beginning or the end of the day. This can be a good way to set yourself up for some good thoughts right away in the morning. Or you can use it to clear out your head from everything that might be bothering you, so you can get to sleep easier. The journal entries don't have to be too long, but just use it as a way to release some of the stress that you already feel during the day.

Some people find that working with yoga and meditation can also help. Both of these can help to clear out the mind and make it easier for you to relax in ways that may have been harder to do otherwise. It is sometimes hard to get started with meditation because your mind may not want to quiet down from all the thoughts you have and the feelings you experience. But over time, you will get better at it, and you will see that meditation can really benefit you.

Do some preparation ahead of time

Sometimes, if you just prepare yourself when you get started, you will be able to see a better comprehension of the material you are working on. This doesn't have to take very long and considering it saves you a lot of time reading the document as a whole, it is definitely worth your time.

The first thing that you should consider doing is taking a look at any summary that comes with the information. You can look at the back cover, the synopsis, or any other summary that comes with this document. This helps you to get an idea beforehand of what is in the document to start with, and some of the main keywords that you are able to work with. It won't go in depth too much, but it can be a great way to give you a general idea of what to look for in the document.

You can also take the time to look at the headings in the document. Look at chapter headings and subheadings. These will pretty much give you an idea of what is in that section of the document before you even start reading. This way, you have a good idea of what to expect and can just search out the terms that are the most important to you as you speed read through it.

Picking out some main keywords that you want to look for in the document ahead of time can be helpful. By looking at the chapter headings and the summary of the document, you should already have a decent list of what you want to look for in keywords. Write these down and keep them nearby. Your eye will be instantly drawn to these words and the ones near them, and this can help you get through the information fast.

If you are just reading a chapter or two in a textbook, take some time to read through the introduction and summary that goes with each one. Most of the information that you need will be found there. You will find the most common topics and key takeaways, and you can search for those as your speed reading to enhance the amount of reading comprehension you have.

Eat something before you start

Focus is one of the main reasons that a lot of people struggle with doing well in speed reading. People will often have something on their mind causing them not to be able to concentrate at all. One of the things that is on peoples minds regular can be a hungry stomach.

When you are hungry, it is hard to concentrate on anything. Not being able to concentrate will effect your reading and comprehension greatly. Before you sit down and work on your speed reading exercises, take some time to eat a small snack or supper if it is that late in the day. You don't want to stuff yourself in this process, but having enough to make the stomach comfortable can help you do well with comprehending what you read. You can instead focus on the words you see in front of you, rather than the rumbling in your stomach.

While reading fast is important and is the main topic of this guide, you also want to make sure that you are actually understanding and comprehending the words you see. You don't have to catch every word, but if you do some speed reading exercises and aren't able to comprehend a single thing that you read on the page, then you need to make some adjustments. Speed reading should help improve your concentration, not hinder it, so make sure to work on some of the tips in this guidebook to see how it can help you with your reading comprehension.

Chapter 7

SUBVOCALIZATION

One of the biggest obstacles to you seeing success with your speed reading is the process of subvocalization. This is known as auditory reassurance. It is when you read through something and then say the words, either by mouthing them or saying them in your head. Your talking speed is much slower than what your mind can process, and if you are limiting yourself to only being able to read as fast as the mind can say the words, then you are going to run into some trouble with increasing your reading speed.

When we were all originally taught how to read, we had to learn how to do it out loud. This allowed the teacher and others to hear if we were saying the words right, so they could help us more to improve and see better results. Then, once we were considered fluent enough, we were told to say the words in our heads as we worked through this. This may be a common way to teach people how to read, but it is the basics of why we say

the words in our head when we read. And this is where the habit of subvocalization is going to originate. It is common for many people to continue on with this habit for the rest of their lives because that is just what they are used to.

While this may be the way that we are used to doing things, if we want to be able to increase our reading speeds, then it is time to minimize this habit as much as possible. It is not necessary to read out every word on a page in our heads just to get an understanding of what is there. Yes, when we were younger, this was a skill to learn and reading the words out loud was necessary to help you learn how to read. But it isn't necessary for you to do this now to extract the meaning of them. In fact, many adults can get the meaning out of these words just by seeing them.

There are many situations when you can read without saying the word in your head at all. You may already be doing it in some way or another in your own personal life. For example, any time that you see a stop sign, you just stop, without reading the words out in your head or out loud. You may read out the word "stop" in a

93

sentence on a page, but for the stop sign, you do not read it out at all. This is the same kind of skill that we want to learn how to use when we read any kind of document.

If you are like other readers, you probably end up subvocalizing all, or at least most, of the words that you read in your head. But you won't always subvocalize everything that you read. An example of this is if you were reading something and came across the year "1788". You probably went through and said, "Seventeen eighty-eight." You are more likely to understand the year by just seeing the number. But if you saw a big number, like 304,003,543,100, then you wouldn't go through and subvocalize all of that.

With the second number, you know that it is a big one, and the understanding of that can come quickly, without you having to go through and subvocalize it. If you did try to subvocalize this, then you would end up spending a ton of time reading through this due to the length of it. You will still get the idea that it is a big number, no matter which way you've done it.

Reading isn't necessarily about the words that you read, but more about extracting ideas, absorbing the information, and getting the details. Individual words all on their own aren't going to mean all that much unless they are surrounded by other words. Being able to group the words together will help you to go faster when you read.

Many of the words that we look at are just there for grammatical purposes, and they don't necessarily add to the meaning of the sentence. These would be words like "the, an, a". They don't provide the same kind of meaning that you will get from other words, and learning how to skip over them and not subvocalize them, will ensure that you are able to read through a document faster and still get the right comprehension from it.

Think about it this way: if you spend your time saying each word out loud in your head, this basically means that you are only able to read as fast as you can talk. While some people can do this a bit faster than others, it still doesn't allow you to get up to the reading speeds that you can find with speed reading, which defeats the purpose of these exercises. If you have to go through and say all the words that you see in your head, then your limit will always be your talking speed, and you will never be able to get through it any faster.

The average reading speed for most people will be somewhere between 150 to 250 words each minute. This is going to be the exact same as for what their talking speed will be. Because most people use subvocalization and say the words in their head, which slows them down. You can test this out on yourself if you are curious. Try doing some reading for one minute normally, and then try to read it out loud for a minute. If you are like most people, you will find that you are going to be pretty similar in both methods.

If you did this exercise and you notice that your reading speed did go more than 50 words a minute faster than the talking speed, then this is a good sign. This means that you are on your way to being able to speed read, because your reading speed isn't held back by your talking speed. If your speeds are about the same, that's fine too. You will be able to work on it and see some improvements.

Subvocalization is one of the most important things that you can work on to help speed up your reading. But changing this habit is much easier said than done. Turning this voice in your head off can be hard. For most people, it is more about minimizing the habit rather than eliminating it completely.

An example of this may be the sentence "The girl tied her shoes." Instead of reading out all of the words there, you could just read "girl tied shoes." This gets the same meaning out of it but cuts down the words, so you can get through it faster. Your eyes will still see the words, so it's not like you are actually skipping them, but it ensures that you read through and subvocalize fewer of them, so you can go through the document much faster. Remembering that a lot of the words that are found in each document are not essential when it comes to the meaning of the content, even if they are essential to the grammar of the documents content. You will just be skipping a lot of what is not needed to get to the overall meaning.

Now that we have taken some time to talk about why subvocalization is bad for you and can slow down your reading speed, there are sometimes when saying the words, you see in your head can be helpful. For example, if the material that you want to tread through has really difficult or technical terminology or information that you are not familiar with, subvocalization can help you get through it a bit easier. In these kinds of situations, saying the words out loud or in your head can help you to understand it better, and can even help you to expand out your own vocabulary.

If you need to memorize something word for word, then working with subvocalization is a great thing as well. How do you think actors are able to remember their own lines for a part? If you did speed reading, you might get the general idea of what the words are saying, but you will never be able to memorize them all. Reading the words out loud can be useful when you are trying to memorize something word for word. But when you do your regular type of reading, you will rarely need to know the whole thing word for word. You just need to read to get the main details, ideas, and information from the document, and this is where speed reading can help.

To help you boost your reading speed, you need to figure out the method that works the best for you to minimize the subvocalization that you have by saying just a few words out of each line. This speeds you up, rather than letting your talking speed be your limit.

But how do you know if your habit of subvocalization is actually changing? If you were to do a test and you find that you are reading over 300 words, especially if you were at just 150 to 200, words per minute, then this is a sign that you have cut down on the number of words that you are saying in your reading because you can't talk that fast. If you find that your reading speed is over 400 words a minute, then you are making a lot of progress, and you have really limited the number of words that you are saying in your head.

Best Ways to Minimize Your Subvocalization

Now that we have spent some time talking about subvocalization and all it means, it is time to look at some of the tools that you can use to minimize the skill as much as possible. The more that you are able to minimize this issue, the easier speed reading will be.

You can tell that you are successful when you do the tests and see that your reading speed is getting faster than your talking speed. Some of the things that you can do to minimize the subvocalization that is going on in your head include:

Use your hand as a guide while reading

This is one of the techniques that we talked about earlier, but it not only helps you keeps pace with reading, but it can help you to reduce the amount of subvocalization that is going on. Your hand can be a great way to help guide your eyes, so you have to move along and not read everything out. You will be able to use your hand, or a pointer or another tool, to guide your eyes. Through this process, since you are forcing yourself through a bit faster and your eyes will focus more on the words that are important.

Find ways to distract yourself

To help minimize this problem with your reading, you can find ways to distract yourself, so you are less likely to say the words in your head. How can you distract yourself during reading? One way is to consider

chewing some gum when you read. This may seem a bit silly, but people find that when they chew gum while reading, it distracts them from saying the words in their head. It has also been proven to help concentration in visual memory tasks.

Another way that you can stop this problem in your head is to use another voice. Some people have success with counting from one to three when they are doing their speed reading. While you do this, focus somewhere at the beginning of the line at one, then the middle for two, and then the end of the line for three. Doing this is going to make it easier to fixate on three groups of words, rather than just looking at each word in the line. You get the choice of saying the numbers and counting out loud or in your head. Either way, you can distract yourself from saying the actual words you are reading. Over time this gets easier, and you will be able to read through the words without saying them in your head.

Listen to some music while you read

Listening to music when you read can help in two ways. First, it is going to minimize the amount of subvocalization that you will have going on during the reading session. And it can help you to increase the amount of concentration you have for the document.

You have to be careful with the type of music you decide to you because not all of them will be effective at helping you concentrate. Don't go with a type of music that has lyrics in it, or any that has a strong beat because these turn your concentration off. You should also avoid any music that may remind you of other things, for this can cause your focus to go off course as you remember all of those memories.

The best bet here is to listen to some music that is instrumental. Most people find that working with classical music can work best for them. It is a soft melody, no lyrics, no strong beat, and it can really help you concentrate, whether you are reading or doing other work during that time. Classical music, or other similar types of music, will help you to improve your concentration right away and can really minimize the subvocalization habit that you have.

Pushing Yourself

You may have to push yourself to read a bit faster instead of just hoping that it will work. Let's say that your normal reading speed is at 250 words per minute. You should try to push yourself to go a little faster as often as you can. You don't need to go crazy, maybe 300 to 350 words per minute if you started at around 250 words per minute. When you take the time to push yourself into saying more words at a faster rate than normal, you will be able to minimize the amount of subvocalization that is going on inside your head.

This happens because you have to improve your focus to get in the extra words. You don't have to go crazy, but just sitting down and trying to push for that little extra speed, can make a world of difference.

There are a lot of different tools out there that you can use to help increase your reading speed. Some of the tools may make exaggerated claims that don't make sense and will be over the top for what you can actually do. But if you add in a lot more practice, and you take care in actually using the right tools, you are going to see some amazing results with how much faster you are able to read.

Chapter 8

Practice Makes Perfect

You are never going to see good results with speed reading if you don't take the time to practice the work and some of the techniques that we have talked about in this guide. It is important to get on a consistent schedule when it comes to working with speed reading. If you can do that, and learn how to push yourself, you will be amazed at how fast your reading speed can improve.

The first thing that you should consider is the best time to do your speed reading and how to practice. If you only practice once a week, or you find that you can only practice here and there, then this is a skill that will falter. Just like with any other skill you choose to obtain, you need to give your speed reading some practice to get better at it. Ideally, try spending at least a little bit of time practicing it each day if you can.

This doesn't mean that you have to spend hours on end practicing your speed reading to get better. In fact, practicing for this long is going to give you a headache and make it impossible to progress any further. You are exercising your brain with this skill, and spending too long on it can make things more difficult to comprehend and stick with. Short sessions, even just fifteen minutes, each day can make a slight difference in the results that you can see.

So, the first step here is to pick a time each day when you can focus on your speed reading endeavors. Schedule it like you would any other important meeting that you need to get done during the week. It only takes about fifteen to twenty minutes, but bringing out your planner and actually writing it down like an important appointment will make it more likely that you will follow and stick with it.

Maybe you find that working on it in the morning, right when you wake up, before the kids get up, is a perfect time. Maybe spending a few minutes during the day when you are on break, or in the evening when things have settled down. You can pick any time that works for you, just make sure that you can maintain your consistency and that you stick with it to enhance this skill.

Another thing that you need to consider is the spot where you would like to do your speed reading. You need to make sure that you find a spot that will enhance rather than hinder your reading and everything that you try to do. You need to find a place that is quiet and free of distractions. So, picking to do this in a loud office or in a coffee shop is not going to be the best idea.

If you have your own spots in your home, such as a bedroom or a small office, then this may an ideal place to read. Make sure that the computer is turned off, the phone is left somewhere else, and you can fully concentrate on the task at hand. If others live in the home with you, try to find some way to occupy them away from you for to ensure you can fully concentrate on the task at hand, rather than being interrupted the whole time.

Ok, so now that we understand that practice is so important to helping you hone your own skills with speed reading, it is important to be prepared when it comes to starting your practice sessions. The first thing to consider here is that you want to sit with comfort. You don't want to pick out a chair that is so comfortable that you will fall asleep in it. But you also don't want to go through and have a chair that is so uncomfortable that you end up spending all of your time thinking about the chair rather than the reading at hand. A good office chair can be a good place to start so that you are comfortable but can still concentrate on the reading that you need to do.

The next thing to consider is how relaxed you are. You don't need to spend time getting so relaxed that you will fall asleep. But if you are angry or stressed out or some other issue that makes your body very uncomfortable and unrelaxed, then you are going to have a lot of trouble with concentration. If you aren't feeling the best or feel overwhelmed or have some other reason that you just can't seem to relax, then it is time to make some changes and figure out how to relax ahead of time.

There are many ways that you can make sure that you relax your body before you get started with speed reading. You can make sure that you have something to eat so you don't feel too hungry. You can take a warm bath to relax. Yoga and meditation can be great ways to relax the mind, get the brain to slow down a bit so you can concentrate on the reading instead of whatever problem is bothering you at the moment.

When you are ready to get started with your speed reading, it is time to prepare your mind to help you in your practice reading sessions. You can have your own routine, but there needs to be something that helps you go from the task that you were in before, to transitioning to the right frame of mind before you start. One method to use is to grab the material that you want to use, close your eyes, and then take three deep breaths before you get started. This can often be enough of a transition to help you feel focused and prepare for the reading for better results.

If you still need a little bit more of a transition to see results, then you may think about what you are doing a bit. After the deep breaths, consider telling yourself that you need to read with a purpose. You aren't sitting down to read with the idea of pleasure or even for business. You are doing it to hone this new skill, so take some time to work on it, rather than just trying to get it done and over with. When you know your purpose from the beginning, it is easier to train the mind to get the results that you want, and your reading speed will instantly improve.

There are a lot of different things that you can choose to read through when you practice your speed reading. You can choose to read things like a magazine article, newspapers, books, documents, emails, and more. You can choose to speed read anything that you would like. One option that works well is to practice with the help of newspaper columns.

Newspaper columns are usually really easy for you to speed read through. Many times, the first few paragraphs are going to have all the information that you need. If you spend just a few minutes or less reading those first few paragraphs, you will get all of the information that is needed in order to take in the article information. Then the rest of the newspaper article is going to contain a few more details, but you can use the information from the beginning to get through it all with just skimming and taking a look at. You won't find anything new or exciting through the end of the article, so it can be skipped, or just skimmed to get the rest of the information that you need. Plus, newspaper columns are really fast reading anyway and you probably already skim through them anyway, so it is a great way to practice.

Of course, you don't have to work with newspaper articles to practice your speed reading. You can choose other options as well based on what you are interested in. It is best to speed read with something that is non-fiction. The way that fiction is set up is a bit different, and is not ideal for speed reading. Working with a nonfiction book is a much better way to ensure that you are working on something that is effective with this skill.

With that in mind, remember that you can choose any kind of nonfiction work that you would like. Think about something that greatly interests you, and then pick out some books that are on this topic. This way, you can enjoy the information that you are reading and can learn something at the same time. Just because you are working on a new skill doesn't mean that you can't have some fun and enjoy what you are doing during the process.

Skimming is another thing that you should work on during your practicing time. We have spent some time talking about skimming and how it can be useful for the speed reading process. With this, practice searching for sentences that are on the page that may have the main idea that should be in the document. You should learn how to do this in a manner that allows you to skip over text that is just filler, that is less interesting, and information that is not as relevant as it could be to the main idea. This can be useful in so many aspects of your life, and being able to increase your speed with skimming can ensure you get all the main parts of the document, without having to waste time with all the extra stuff.

When you work on speed reading, you need to make sure that you are practicing all of the different techniques that we talked about before. Many of them can be effective and can help you get faster, but one of the best options is to learn how to guide your reading with a pointer or your finger. This is one of the most

effective methods for speeding up your reading, and if you haven't tried it out, you should give it a chance for at least one practice session. This is something that will help greatly if you run into any problems while trying to speed read.

The method is so simple - you just use a finger or some kind of pointer, like a pen, to help guide the eyes. You can use this pointer to decide how fast you should be reading at. If you want to slow down, move the pointer at a slower speed. If you want to move faster, then you move the pointer a bit faster. You don't have to limit yourself to making movements across the page just going left to right.

Sometimes, you can increase the reading speed even more if you move the pointer in different shapes across the page. Using a finger or a pen to make some of these shapes on the page can help speed up the visual cortex, allowing your visual span to increase, so you learn how to take in a whole line at a time rather than just one or two word. It also makes it easier to imprint the information that you read to the subconscious mind to look at later. It also can help with subvocalization, so it is definitely something to consider when you are working on your speed reading.

Another thing that you may want to work on is how to use the skills and tools of the brain more effectively so that it can go through and read faster. There are already some maps that exist inside the brain that help you to recognize words and understand what is going on around you. If you are able to get these to be more efficient, you will find that it is easier to move through the familiar concepts and words that you see on the page at a much faster rate than before.

If you ever come up against some content that is a bit unfamiliar to you, then make sure that you give it its proper due and really learn it. This helps you to form those strong maps in the brain a bit better. The more that you learn these topics, the easier it is for you to prove the information quickly later on. It will then get imprinted on the brain, and the next time that you read about it, you can skim through it and speed read through it without any problems at all.

You can also practice some of the different things that we discussed in this guidebook in your daily life, even

when it isn't one of your regular practice sessions. For example, the next time that you see a signboard outside of a restaurant or another store in your area, glance at it and then look away. Were you able to recall what was on it? If you are just starting with speed reading, you probably can't read through it very well. But after some practice, you will be able to do this with just a glance at anything, and reading a sign with a glance and comprehending what is on it will seem like nothing at all.

Some of the other things that you should consider trying out when it is time to work on your speed reading include:

> **Keep the harmful distractions out of the way:** Reading faster is always about maximizing your concentration as much as possible. So, make sure that you are able to support this goal. Keep the designated area free of any noisy electronic devices, like your video games, your television, your computer, your phone, or anything else that could keep your mind away from what you want to accomplish. If the area

already functions as a study space, then this should already be set up well for you. But you can use any room that you want for this process, just make sure that you hide away anything that is going to cause distractions and issues for you.

Learn how to eliminate the problem with regression: Regression is basically the process of re-reading the same passages over again. Doing this even just once during the session can slow you down a lot. This is often due to lack of concentration, but many different issues can come into play here. You need to learn how to stop this to increase your speed. Working in three to four-word clusters of words, working with skimming, and using something that blocks the passages you have read, such as a piece of paper, so you are forced to move forward and not go backward can be something that works well.

Increase your eye movements: There are several exercises that you can work with that will boost your eye movements, and can make it easier to read faster. One method that you can work on is to read a first paragraph or passage at a normal speed for a minute. Then read it three additional times, but have your index finger move you along the page. Double and triple your reading speeds each time you do this. During the additional times, focus on some of the keywords to help you with comprehension as well. This can help you to move the rate at which your eyes read the words, and can help in so many ways later on when it comes to your reading speed.

➤ **Figure out ways to minimize the amount of subvocalization:** This is the single biggest thing that is going to cause you to slow down with your reading speed. You need to learn how to turn this off, or you are always going to be limited to your talking speed when it comes to your reading speed. We have discussed a lot of ways that you can limit your subvocalization, but during your practice sessions, make sure that you try out a few of these as well.

➤ **Vary your reading speeds:** Before you get started, you should consider the different intellectual demands of any kind of material that you choose to read. You can then adjust the speed to match. If you are reading an entertainment article for fun, you can definitely read through it much faster than reading on a topic about programming. A good reader is able to figure out the overall complexity of the information, and then they determine how much time they need to spend on the content. Sometimes they are able to skim over it, and other times they know they need to spend more time on it to get the information that they need.

Setting some time aside to help you learn how to speed read can be so important to ensure that you see the results that you want. You are never going to get better with your reading if you just work on it occasionally or you never work with it at all. Use the tips in this chapter to set up a good time and routine for practicing that you can maintain and stick with on a consistent basis, and you will find that your reading speed will increase in no time at all.

Chapter 9

Speed Reading Studies

This guide has spent a lot of time talking about speed reading and why it can be so great for your overall professional and personal life. We have shown that there are a lot of benefits that come with speed reading, and being able to read through things much faster can be really helpful when it comes to getting through documents and other literature as quickly as possible. But how much truth is there when it comes to speed reading? Is this actually something that works? Are you actually able to learn how to read quickly and go from about 200 words per minute to over 1000 words per minute? This chapter is going to take a look at, and shed some light on some of the studies for speed reading.

Be Careful with Sites that Try to Sell You Speed Reading Programs

There are a lot of people who want to be able to learn how to speed read, and also be able to learn to do it in a short period of time. They want to receive all of the benefits that come with speed reading without having to spend weeks doing it. Because of the increased interest in speed reading, there are a lot of companies out there who will make big promises, like getting you to increase your word count in no time at all, often with time limits that don't make sense compared to the level you are at.

These companies will state that they can help you increase your reading speed in just a few weeks, taking you from 200 words to 500 words in that time, and then to an even higher level straight afterwards. This may sound like a great deal, but honestly, this is way more than what most people can do, and the amount that they charge you is going to be outrageous. Considering that you can increase your reading speed with your finger and some reading material that you find online, there is no reason that you should spend hundreds of dollars letting someone else "tell" you how to do it.

Learning the basics of speed reading may seem like one of the best strategies for making quick work of reports emails, and other texts that we need to encounter each day. But there has now been a comprehensive review of the science that is behind reading, and it shows that the claims that are put out there by quite a few reading programs and tools are often too good to be true. This review took time to look over the research that was done over a decade about the science of reading. Through this, a team of psychological scientists found that there is little evidence that speed reading is a shortcut to understanding and remembering larger volumes of written content in a short amount of time.

The scientists state that the training courses for speed reading have been around for a long period, and they have found that there is a recent surge in how many technologies are now available for speed reading. The point of the study was to take a closer look at the science that is behind reading and look to see whether or not the technologies and the paid programs were actually able to increase speed reading and if this could benefit your comprehension. According to Elizabeth Schotter, a psychological scientist at the University of California, San Diego, "We wanted to take a close look at the science behind reading to help people make informed decisions about whether to believe the claims put forth by companies promoting speed reading technologies and training courses." This is the reason that the review was done in the first place.

This particular report was published by Psychological Science in the Public Interest to take a look at how great speed reading works and if it can benefit you. This study found that speed reading could be beneficial to helping you get through larger amounts of text quickly, and when it is used properly, you will be able also to comprehend the information better. But, many of the techniques that are used by the big companies trying to sell their products and technologies make promises that just aren't realistic, and most people are disappointed and frustrated by the results that they get.

Reading is considered a complex dance with a few different visual and mental processes, and researchers have found that many skilled readers are already reading through things pretty quickly on their own, averaging between 200 and 400 words per minute. But there are some speed reading technologies will make claims that say that those who use their technologies will be able to boost the speed seven times more because they are able to eliminate the need to make eye movements by presenting the user with words quickly on the phone or computer screen.

The issue with this is that the eye movements that you use are only going to account for about ten percent of the time, overall, that you spend reading. By eliminating the ability to go back and reread previous words and sentences tends to make comprehension worse, rather than better in many cases. The biggest obstacle with how fast we can read, according to science, isn't really in our vision and our eye movements, but in how well we are able to recognize the words on the page, and the processes that we use to combine those words to make meaningful sentences.

However, even though the speed reading technologies are not going to really be able to help you increase the speed that you are able to read at, you will find that skimming can be a really effective method to help you out. In fact, research has found that the people who are the most effective at speed reading are actually effective at skimming. This can be even more effective when you have a little bit of understanding and familiarity with the topic at hand, which means that they are able to find the right keywords and get through the information a bit faster.

Another thing that can help with boosting how well you are able to read through a topic is practicing your reading for comprehension. Greater exposure to writing, no matter what kind of form it is in, can help you to have a larger and richer vocabulary. It can also help you learn more contextual experience that is going to help you to anticipate upcoming words based on what you are already reading, so you can then get through the material faster.

No matter what, it is healthy to have a bit of skepticism when it comes to speed reading and what may or may not work for you. There are a lot of programs out there that claim they can increase your reading speed in no time. Some of them may be able to help. But you can also work with increasing your speed reading all on your own without the help of other tools, and without having to pay out a lot of money to get it done either. Always being a skeptic and picking out the program that works the best for your needs is the best option to go with.

Additional Studies about Speed Reading

There have been numerous studies done on speed reading and whether or not it is an effective tool in helping you to comprehend more and see the best results with getting things done. One study shows that the maximum that we can read, without skipping any of the words that are on the page, is about 500 words a minute. This assumes that there is no backtracking either, although about fifteen percent of the time that we spend reading is going to be for regressions. It also assumes that there isn't much comprehension beyond identifying the words. But in practice, studies have shown that most of us are going to be able to read around 250 words a minute.

Of course, remember that with most of the methods of speed reading that we do, we aren't going to spend our time reading each and every word. Most of the words on the page are there for grammatical reasons, rather than for the meaning or for comprehension. So, we can already speed up beyond that 500 words just by figuring out which words aren't necessary and learning how to skip them.

Another study that we need to look at is one that shows that reading faster than 500 words can be possible. However, a lot of these studies need to change up the way they conduct the survey and the research that bring them more into the mainstream. For example, one of these studies found that after participants spend 16 hours doing training for speed reading, they would be able to read at a significantly faster speed than before. This shows that speed training can be effective; however, there weren't any control groups in the study, so it is possible the participants were just able to become familiarized with the experimental procedure from one test to the other, or they had reading materials that were a bit easier the second time they did the test.

Other studies are also going to boast impressive improvements, but they are going to rely on a device that is known as a tachistoscope. What this is, is a tool that is going to flash the words on a screen for briefer and briefer periods of time until the person is able to read through them very quickly, but this isn't the same as being actually able to read through the material. Without this tool, the readers found that it was difficult to go back to regular reading and see results, making it very ineffective.

About ten years ago, Keith Rayner, a psychologist and one of the most widely respected experts in the field on what the eyes are doing when we read, was able to pinpoint one single study of speed reading as both rigorous and interpretable. Inside of this study, psychologists spent time monitoring how the eyes moved for speed readers, or readers who were able to take in 600 to 700 words per minute, and the eye movements of those who were considered normal readers, or who could read 250 words a minute.

In this study, the researchers determined that those who were speed readers were able to move their eyes more quickly because they didn't make as many fixations as the other readers did. Instead of reading through each and every word that was in the document, they were able to read a few words here and there.

Another interesting thing about this study is that the researchers tested those who did speed reading and found that these readers did pretty well on general questions, just from the basics that they read through the document and some of the pre-existing knowledge that they had on the document itself. But when they were tested on the little details of the text, they missed out and often did poorly here.

This is close to what we already know happens with speed reading. This is meant to give you the basis of a topic and can help you with some conversation starters or getting things done with the information, but you aren't going to be able to list off a ton of details about it. If you need to read through a document and get all the information out of it, or you know it is a technical or new topic, then you will need to slow down, as we have already discussed earlier.

We also took a look at how your eye fixations need to be limited when you speed read. This helps you to make fewer stops when you are reading, and it can help you to see faster results than usual. This is what was seen in the study. Speed readers were able to go through the text at a much faster rate because they didn't stop at each and every word like normal readers would do.

In this same study, the researchers asked the normal readers to skim the text and see if they were able to get to 600 to 700 words a minute. These skimmers eye movements and their results on comprehension tests ended up being about the same as the speed readers. This shows that you definitely don't need to spend a ton of money on a speed reading seminar to get results. You just need to be able to read through and skim the text, with a bit of practice of your own, to increase your reading speed.

What is really amazing out of this is that it is believed that some people are able to read up to 2500 words a minute, but none of them have been tested yet to see how this works and how their comprehension is during this. These individuals may be a little above what most of us can do and perhaps have more of a photographic memory, where they are able to just glance at the page and remember everything that is on it. Since most of us are not able to have this skill and a photographic memory isn't something that you can gain with practice, it is something that you are born with, we may just have to deal with the slower reading speeds and work on seeing if we can make them a little faster to help us out.

Knowing When to Slow Down

Now, there are many different reasons why you would want to learn how to speed read. It can make reading more enjoyable because no one wants to spend hours trying to get through even the most basic of topics. You will find that it helps you get your work done because you are able to actually get through it all and move on, rather than just concentrating on the reading. It can help you to do better when you speak to others and when you need to communicate with them better because you have the right information to converse and not feel nervous along the way.

Even with all of the good things that come with speed reading, experts and studies alike will bring up the point that it is a good idea to learn when its best to slow down on things. Speed reading can be done with a wide variety of materials. You will find that it works well with newspaper articles, magazines, some nonfiction books, and other materials that you may already have some familiarity with. But for those brand new topics or the ones that are more technical and harder to work with, you will find that it may be better to slow down a bit.

This isn't to discourage you from reading fast and seeing how much you can build up this skill. But your comprehension will struggle in some cases. Speed reading isn't always the biggest problem with this because with regular reading your focus is going to drift off and comprehension can go down, while this is less likely to happen when you are speed reading. But still, you will find that comprehension can often lack when you are working on a more complex subject.

What this means is if you are working on some sort of tough or complex material, go ahead and slow down. If you are studying for a psychology test and you know nothing about psychology, then slow down. If you are learning a new language and trying to figure out some of the rules that go with it, then slow down when reading. Any time that the subject may seem a little bit difficult for you to handle, or you don't understand how it works at all, then take a slower approach to reading it.

This doesn't mean that you can't use some of the techniques that we have talked about in this guide to help you read faster. These can still be utilized and will ensure that you are able to get through the material faster than normal. But, you should slow down and not try to speed through things when you are first learning them or if you find them difficult at all.

Speed reading has captured the attention of a lot of people over the years. Many people are interested in learning how to master speed reading to improve many different aspects of their life, both professionally and personally. Whether you want to use it to help improve your communication skills with others or because you want to speed through the work that needs to be done, working with speed reading can be a great way to get started.

CONCLUSION

Thanks for making it through to the end of *this book*. Let's hope it was informative and able to provide you with all of the tools you need to achieve your goals whatever they may be.

The next step is to put some of these techniques into practice and see how it can work for you. While many think that speed reading can be a difficult thing to work on, it is actually pretty easy and fun. You just need to make sure that you pick a technique that you find effective, and then maintain some steady practice with it. But don't be shy when it comes to trying different techniques, some may be for you and some may not.

This guide has took some time to discuss the different ways that you can get started with speed reading in your own life. We have looked at the benefits of speed reading, some of the techniques that you can use, how to stop the problem of subvocalization, and how to increase your comprehension at the same time. When you put all of these lessons into practice you will be able to increase your reading speed and see some amazing results.

It may take some time for you to find your edge, but eventually you will get there, and you will be speed reading like a pro

Finally, if you found this book useful in any way, a review on Amazon is always appreciated!

DESCRIPTION

Are you ready to get your work done in just minutes, rather than taking hours to pour over information before you can even get started? Are you interested in learning more information in a shorter amount of time to do better with conversations and interacting with other people? Would you like to make reading more enjoyable, whether it is for work or for fun?

Speed reading can make all of this happen and more! With the techniques that are discussed in this guidebook, you will learn how to increase your speed effectively, helping you to get the results that you want in no time at all. Some of the topics that we will discuss in this guidebook concerning speed reading include:

- ➤ What is speed reading?
- ➤ Calculating your personal reading speed.
- ➤ How to read faster and see your speed during your reading.
- ➤ Where people go wrong when they are trying to speed read.

- How to increase your comprehension and get more out of your speed reading sessions.
- The problem with subvocalization and how to prevent it.
- How practice can help you get even better with your speed reading.
- Some studies on speed reading and how it can improve your professional and personal life.

Speed reading is one of the best skills that you can teach yourself to make reading more enjoyable, help yourself learn more information in a short amount of time, and even get more work done. When you are ready to learn all the tips and tricks to making speed reading work for you, check out this guidebook to get started.

CPSIA information can be obtained
at www.ICGtesting.com
Printed in the USA
BVHW031211070819
555308BV00001B/267/P

9 781913 327040